ERIC/OSEP
Mini-Library

Adapting
Curricular
Materials

D0053570

Toward Successful Inclusion of Students with Disabilities: The Architecture of Instruction

Edward J. Kame'enui and
Deborah C. Simmons

Published by
The Council for Exceptional Children

A Product of the
ERIC/OSEP Special Project
The ERIC Clearinghouse on
Disabilities and Gifted Education

Library of Congress Cataloging-in-Publication Data

Kameenui, Edward J.
    Toward successful inclusion of students with disabilities : the architecture of instruction : an overview of curricular adaptations / Edward J. Kame'enui and Deborah C. Simmons.
        p. cm. — (Adapting curricular materials ; v. 1)
    Includes bibliographical references (p.).
    ISBN 0-86586-338-5 (paper)
        1. Inclusive education—United States. 2. Handicapped students—Education—United States—Curricula. 3. Curriculum change—United States. I. Simmons, Deborah C. II. Title. III. Series.
    LC1201.K36 1999
    371.9'046—dc21   99-12955
                                                                                          CIP

ISBN 0-86586338-5

A product of the ERIC/OSEP Special Project, the ERIC Clearinghouse on Disabilities and Gifted Education.

Published in 1999 by The Council for Exceptional Children, 1920 Association Drive, Reston, Virginia 20191-1589

Stock No. P5305

This publication was prepared with funding from the U.S. Department of Education, Office of Special Education Programs, contract no. ED-99-CO-0026. Contractors undertaking such projects under government sponsorship are encouraged to express freely their judgment in professional and technical matters. Prior to publication the manuscript was submitted for critical review and determination of professional competence. This publication has met such standards. Points of view, however, do not necessarily represent the official view or opinions of either The Council for Exceptional Children or the Department of Education.

Printed in the United States of America
10 9 8 7 6 5 4 3 2 1

Contents

Preface

Teachers in inclusive classrooms regularly face the difficult task of having to modify the curriculum to reach all of their students, many of whom have special needs. Students with disabilities, whether physical, emotional, or cognitive in nature, respond to the curriculum differently from other students. For example, depending on the disability itself and other factors affecting their ability to succeed academically, students may need modifications such as advance and graphic organizers, instructional scaffolding, additional practice and time to complete assignments, and/or alternative media (e.g., large-print materials, audiotapes, or electronic materials). Without specific modifications, the standard curricular materials can be inadequate for these students, and too frequently they can find themselves blocked from access to essential aspects of the curriculum. Teachers must adjust the materials or their presentation to break down the barriers and assist these students in learning.

The IDEA Amendments of 1997 require that students with disabilities have access to the general education curriculum. This legislative requirement makes the accessibility of curricular materials an issue of even greater importance than it otherwise would be. To meet the goal of equal access to the curriculum for everyone, to enable each student to engage with his or her lessons in a meaningful way, teachers must be prepared to provide useful alternatives in terms of both curricular materials and instructional delivery. Well-adapted materials without an effective method of teaching are practically useless, but with the proper tools and instructional methods, a good teacher encourages each member of the class to participate directly in the learning experience.

Unfortunately, teachers who have to work with standard, off-the-shelf curricular materials usually have little time to develop accommodations for their classes. They need a guidebook that outlines successful adaptation strategies in clear, concise language, something that demonstrates the link between purpose and procedure for a teacher in a classroom of diverse learners. This ERIC/OSEP Mini-Library was designed to fill the gap for educators who are already engaged in curriculum adaptations as well as those who have not yet begun. The three volumes in this series

- Outline the conceptual strategies behind instructional adaptations.
- Present characteristics of classroom materials that allow for effective adaptations.
- Illustrate those adaptations in brief, process-oriented chapters and vignettes. The adaptations describe best or promising practices that are based upon relevant special education research.

The Mini-Library consists of three books:

1. An introductory overview on general principles of adaptation of curricular materials, written by Edward J. Kame'enui and Deborah Simmons of the University of Oregon.
2. A volume on adaptation for kindergarten through fifth grade, using the content areas of reading and math, by Jeanne Shay Schumm of the University of Miami.
3. A volume on adaptation in grades three through eight, in language arts, social studies, and science, by Jean Schumaker and Keith Lenz of the University of Kansas.

Clearly, three short volumes cannot cover the range of disabilities and other diverse learning needs that teachers have to confront. We have limited our consideration to mild cognitive disabilities and have focused on adapting materials rather than on delivery (although in practice the two go hand in hand). For those who wish to read more about adaptations, the books provide references to additional resources on effective teaching methods and research.

A Word on Universal Design

This Mini-Library proceeds from the assumption that teachers who have to adapt instruction for their students usually don't have a say in choosing the curriculum or designing the materials before they are expected to use them. This series of publications offers the means to facilitate that process. If the developers of curricular materials anticipated some of the needs that teachers face in inclusive classrooms, such as students who read below grade level or who have organizational or attention-deficit problems, and if they then designed accommodations for these needs into the materials, that would free up teachers to devote more time to teaching and less to adapting the curriculum. While this may sound like an ideal situation, actually it is neither unrealistic nor far in the future of public school classrooms. Over the past few years, there has been a concerted effort in special education to promote curricular materials with built-in adaptations, particularly in digital media, that are flexible and customizable. Known as *universal design for learning,* the movement is based on the principles behind the universal design movement for access to products and environments for all users, regardless of sensory or physical disabilities.

The educational strategies behind universal design for learning basically underlie any sort of classroom adaptations. When a teacher adapts a curriculum, she or he works to accommodate as many student needs as possible by developing an array of potential supports. An unadapted curriculum generally is one-size-fits-all, but adapted materials can be tailored to the students. In this way, universally designed materials can accommodate students where they need it, but those supports are incorporated during the development phase, rather than having to be added after the fact. The same strategies that teachers use to adapt inefficient or inconsiderate materials go into universally designed curricular materials. A history text, for example, is written to include graphic organizers and strategic questions to help students who would find a typical text inaccessible but also to provide a challenge for those who would otherwise find it boring or unengaging. A digital reading program can highlight the text word for word or sentence by sentence for students who have difficulty following along by themselves, or it can say the words out loud for those who need more familiarity with the sounds of what they read. Such adaptations could be designed and provided by teachers—and this Mini-Library provides a number of successful examples—but the more resources that come packaged with the curriculum, the greater its flexibility and the less it has to be modified by the teacher.

Although materials that incorporate aspects of universal design have yet to become routine in schools, school districts in several states already are using preadapted books and digital media in their classrooms. For example, under a Department of Education grant, the Center for Applied Special Technology (CAST) is currently working with the State of New Hampshire to study the potential of technology to promote literacy for all students. This project, now implemented in 16 New England schools, uses a CD-ROM-based instructional program, *WiggleWorks,* that employs principles of universal design for learning. Other states, such as Texas and California, are using such preadapted, technology-supported programs for curriculum delivery. As technology inevitably plays an increasingly central instructional role, the concept of universal design for learning will gain prominence.

A Final Word on Adaptations

No computer or other classroom tool, no adapted materials can ever take the place of the teacher. Without an informed and dedicated teacher directing the learning, without someone who knows the students well enough to know what barriers to break down and where and how much to challenge a student, then even the best tools will be useless. Universally designed and adapted curricular materials are intended to provide teachers with more time and better means to get the job done, not to do the job for them.

Acknowledgments

Many people contribute their invaluable time and skills to a project such as this, and they need to be acknowledged. This Mini-Library resulted from a need to update a popular publication on curricular adaptations developed 10 years ago by the ERIC/OSEP Special Project. In late 1997, the Special Project, under the aegis of and with the support of the Office of Special Education Projects (OSEP), convened a group of researchers and practitioners to discuss the best ways to address the need for adapted materials in the inclusive classroom. Those intensive discussions and subsequent suggestions resulted in the outline for this series of books. We extend our appreciation to the researchers and teachers involved in the initial stages of this project and to authors Kame'enui, Lenz, Schumaker, Schumm, and Simmons, who agreed to devote a large portion of their time to this project in addition to their regular duties. We hope this Mini-Library will be a valuable tool for both special and general educators.

The manuscripts were graciously and carefully reviewed by a number of practitioners and researchers in the field. Their comments helped us to help the authors tighten the expression of their ideas. Special thanks are extended to Louise Appel, Pamela Burrish, Russell Gersten, Kathy Haagenson, Pauletta King, John Lloyd, Patricia Mathes, and Elba Reyes.

Special appreciation goes to Lou Danielson, director of OSEP's Research to Practice Division, whose commitment to these activities is borne out by his participation at each stage of development. The staff of the ERIC/OSEP Special Project at The Council for Exceptional Children were responsible for the meeting described previously and for conceptualizing and editing the three volumes. They are Kathleen McLane, Ray Orkwis, and Jane Burnette. All of us involved in developing these materials hope you will find them useful in your work, and we welcome your responses.

Nancy Safer
Executive Director
The Council for Exceptional Children

1

Introduction:
From Physical to Cognitive
Access—Building Cognitive
Ramps and Scaffolds

Today, gaining physical access to schools and classrooms for students with disabilities is no longer the legal issue it was more than 20 years ago. For all practical purposes, students with disabilities now have ready and deliberate access to schools and to general education classrooms. In the short span of 2 decades since the passage of Public Law 94-142 (the Education for All Handicapped Children Act of 1975), special education has moved beyond merely gaining physical access to general education schools and classrooms. Kauffman and Hallahan (1997) argued that "[access] also involves the methods, materials, and equipment used in instruction, the particular students being taught, the teacher or teachers who provide instruction, and the tasks students are asked to perform" (p. 336).

Simply providing physical access to general education does not ensure that students with disabilities will gain cognitive access to the content of the general education curriculum. For these students to gain cognitive access to general education content, attention must be given to the "architectural" requirements of the general education content. Furthermore, to provide students with disabilities a reasonable chance of being successful with this content, we must find effective ways to make the content accessible, memorable, and sustainable.

Providing cognitive access to curriculum materials is akin to creating a ramp that provides physical access to a building for a student in a wheelchair. For physical access to the building, the ramp must be specially designed for that particular building; using a standard ramp simply will not do. Minimum criteria for ramps are applied to the particular building to which access is needed. Some buildings require greater adaptations than others, depending on specific features.

Likewise, the cognitive "ramps" that allow students to gain access to the curriculum must be geared to the architecture of the information—the particular characteristics of what is to be learned. Specifically, educators and developers of educational tools must begin by adhering to minimum criteria for well-designed curricula and instruction. Although minimum criteria cannot address the needs of the full range of learners—just as a standard ramp design cannot provide access to all buildings—they can ensure that the majority of students have access to the information to be learned. For a small percentage of students, further adaptation of the curriculum may be necessary for access to the general education content.

Modifying and adapting instructional materials are unavoidable because no one educational tool is accessible to, and usable by, all students, regardless of ability. Many educational tools, however, fail to reflect what we know about basic instructional design and effective instruction. Toward that end, if we intend for all students with disabilities to gain cognitive access to general education content, these cognitive ramps and scaffolds must first be made accessible to general and special education teachers, curriculum specialists, and other stakeholders charged with the design and delivery of instruction to all children. The greater their awareness and working knowledge of these architectural features of well-designed curricula and instruction, the better use these stakeholders can make of these resources and the greater the likelihood that students with disabilities will gain genuine access to curricular content.

Focus of the Book

The primary focus of this book is on designing the cognitive supports to instructional materials for students with disabilities in general education classrooms. The placement of these students presupposes that the content and cognitive outcomes of the general education curriculum are attainable and appropriate for them. In a sense, teachers, administrators, curriculum specialists, and developers and publishers of curriculum materials must know how to package the information to be taught so that all students can successfully obtain, rehearse, recall, apply, and transfer the newly learned information to both routine and novel learning contexts. The fundamental principles of instructional design detailed here should be known by all educators concerned with making information more accessible to all students, particularly those with disabilities.

In this chapter we describe the contexts of change, including the changing demography of learners, which in part has increased the curricular and instructional complexity that teachers face in general education classrooms. In Chapter 2 we define and describe curriculum design as an important and distinctive requirement to providing cognitive access to general education content. In Chapter 3, we describe six principles of "effective curriculum design" that we consider essential to the modification of general education content. These six principles provide teachers with a "blueprint" for designing and developing cognitive ramps and scaffolds to allow students with disabilities cognitive access to the general education content. In Chapter 4, we (a) offer a framework for evaluating and adapting general education curriculum materials and (b) apply the six curriculum design principles to a range of general education content, including the areas of beginning reading and writing.

Student Diversity and Instructional Complexity

The typical public school classroom has changed dramatically in the last few decades, and a growing number of students, including those with disabilities, may not be acquiring basic academic skills and strategies. Never before have the demographics of an individual classroom presented such a diversity of demands on teachers and the core curriculum. Teachers may find themselves overwhelmed trying to meet the needs of such diverse learners, particularly in the face of growing class size and reduced instructional support. Factors such as social problems, poverty, and deteriorating family structure further complicate the problems. Consequently, the traditional curriculum and traditional instructional methods are unlikely to address these problems and meet the diverse needs of the students. It is now more important than ever to examine the role of curriculum design when trying to understand why general or unspecialized instruction may be failing our students. This volume describes how properly designed instructional tools can be used to increase the probability that information in general education classrooms will be learned by students with diverse learning needs.

2

Curriculum Design, Symbolic (Cognitive) Information, and Curriculum Access

Although there are many ways to adapt instruction (e.g., increasing time, presenting information auditorily, reducing the amount or size of the task, all of which are considered in the other volumes of this series), the focus of adaptation here is on the architecture of information, or the curriculum design. Curriculum design refers to the way in which information in a particular area (e.g., social studies, science, reading, mathematics) is selected, prioritized, sequenced, organized, and scheduled for instruction.

Symbolic and Nonsymbolic Information

To appreciate the intricate nature of designing cognitive access to symbolic information, we first have to understand the distinction between symbolic and nonsymbolic information—in other words, the distinction between information needed for cognitive tasks and information needed for motor tasks. Almost all learning and curricula (e.g., reading, mathematics, social studies, science) require students to manipulate, acquire, retain, transform, and recall symbolic information. In contrast, nonsymbolic information requires them to learn physical or motor tasks, such as picking up a pencil, shooting a basketball, or running and jumping.

TABLE 1
Distinction Between Symbolic and Nonsymbolic Information

Symbolic Information Example: Reading the word cup	Nonsymbolic Information Example: Picking up a cup
1. Learning processes are covert and cannot be seen (e.g., silently reading a page of the textbook). Only final outcomes can be observed. *The phonological, linguistic, and cognitive processes implicated in reading the word cup are not readily observable.*	1. Learning processes are overt and can be seen. *The steps in picking up a cup are public and can be observed. It is not possible to pick up a cup without observing the entire act or physical process.*
2. Skills related to a task are sometimes difficult to identify and demonstrate. *The skills implied by the act of reading may vary greatly, depending on a student's cognitive abilities and perspective about reading in an alphabetic writing system.*	2. Skills related to a task are easy to identify and demonstrate. *The steps in picking up a cup follow a particular sequence and involve a limited set of physical acts (e.g., gripping the cup, holding it tightly, picking it up, etc.).*
3. Feedback is not obvious in the execution of the task. *A beginning reader must get feedback from the teacher or other individuals to tell whether his or her comprehension is accurate.*	3. Feedback is instantaneous and obvious in the execution of the task. *To see whether a learner has picked up the cup correctly, one needs only to observe the action and the final response.*

Table 1 identifies three critical differences between symbolic and nonsymbolic information (Kame'enui & Simmons, 1990). The first two component parts of physical tasks (i.e., the learning processes and the demonstrable skills) are always public, observable, and easier to identify than those of symbolic tasks, and the third component (i.e., feedback) is more immediate and transparent than is feedback on a symbolic task.

By initially designing symbolic tasks in ways that make the component skills more overt, a teacher can better gauge whether students are learning the tasks and can then provide them with immediate practice and feedback on their developing skills (Kame'enui & Simmons, 1990, pp. 63–64).

For example, we can simplify the complex task of beginning reading in an alphabetic writing system by

1. Providing students with a clear model of the speech sounds for each letter of the alphabet.

2. Requiring students to say the sounds of each letter in simple word types such as *sat, ran,* and *tot.*

3. Having students "sound out" or decode the words.

4. Then having them read each word the "fast way."

This process relates the symbolic information (i.e., students learning to understand what they are reading) to nonsymbolic, physical skills (i.e., students verbally demonstrating what they are learning).

Curriculum design is the behind-the-scenes activity that appears as the sequence of objectives, schedule of tasks, components of instructional strategies, amount and kind of review, number of examples, amount of teacher direction, and support explicated in teachers' guides and lesson plans. It is the blueprint for instruction. As such, it can hold significant potential for teaching students with diverse learning needs. Conversely, if the blueprint is too general or vague, it can provide little instructional specification or an inadequate foundation on which students are to build further skills and future learning success. For example, consider the following directions modified from a current commercial reading program:

> Have children look at the illustration of a farm in the picture and identify some of the animals. Elicit the word *dog* and write it on the board. Tell children they will learn about the sound they hear at the beginning of *dog* and the letter that stands for that sound. Ask children to read the first line of the story. Have them find the word *dog* and match it with the word on the board. Then, as you read the words ask children to tell which word in the pair begins with the same beginning sound as *dog.*

While this excerpt may seem like an appropriate exercise in beginning reading, the activity makes far too many assumptions about learner preskills, promotes inefficient and ineffective strategies, and relegates teaching to an assessment function only. Moreover, for individuals who have not been prepared to evaluate the architectural features of a curriculum, the more subtle design problems of the activity (e.g., selection and sequence of examples, scaffolded assistance for students to ease into a complex problem) may go unnoticed, although the effects on learners are likely to become evident in their inability to perform the associated tasks that convey their understanding.

Given the importance of curriculum design in preempting learning problems, how can a teacher evaluate a curriculum to determine whether the instructional tool has structured information so that it is memorable, manageable, and meaningful for students with diverse learning needs? To answer these questions, we recommend consideration of six principles that the National Center to Improve the Tools of Educators (NCITE) uses as minimum criteria for evaluating the design or architecture of curricula. They do not represent a definitive guide to developing, selecting, or modifying curricula; rather, they are a starting point for evaluating and selecting instructional tools.[1]

[1]*Access to Curriculum: Instructional Tools for Students with Learning Difficulties.* (1996). Eugene: University of Oregon. (ERIC Document Reproduction Service No. ED 402 723)

3
Six Principles of
Effective Curriculum Design

Summary of the Principles

The six instructional principles described in this chapter can guide teachers as they design tools to promote learning for students with disabilities and diverse learning needs. All too often, tools designed for the majority of students fail to accommodate the unique characteristics and needs of those who require alternative means to access the curriculum (e.g., Kame'enui & Simmons, 1990; Simmons & Kame'enui, 1996.) Table 2 summarizes the critical dimensions of the six principles that serve as minimum criteria for evaluating and adapting instruction and materials. Detailed explanations and examples of each principle follow.

I. Big Ideas

The first and most essential adaptation is determining what information is most critical for students to learn and adjusting the instructional emphasis of the program. We refer to these instructional priorities as *big ideas*. For students in general and students with disabilities in particular, the sheer amount of information in the general education curriculum imposes extraordinary demands on learning.

The growing amount of information to be learned is a source of heavy pressure on educators. As Longstreet and Shane (1993) reported

TABLE 2
Summary of the Critical Dimensions
of the Six Curricular Design Principles

Principle	Criteria/Feature
I. Big Ideas Concepts, principles, or heuristics that facilitate the most efficient and broad acquisition of knowledge	• Focus on essential learning outcomes • Capture rich relationships among concepts • Enable learners to apply what they learn in varied situations • Involve ideas, concepts, principles, and rules central to higher-order learning • Form the basis for generalization and expansion
II. Conspicuous Strategies Useful steps for accomplishing a goal or task	• Planned • Purposeful • Explicit • Of medium-level application • Most important in initial teaching of concept
III. Mediated Scaffolding Instructional guidance provided by teachers, peers, materials, or tasks	• Varied according to learner needs or experiences • Based on task (not more than learner needs) • Provided in the form of tasks, content, and materials • Removed gradually according to learner proficiency
IV. Strategic Integration Integrating knowledge as a means of promoting higher-level cognition	• Combines cognitive components of information • Results in a new and more complex knowledge structure • Aligns naturally with information (i.e., is not "forced") • Involves meaningful relationships among concepts • Links essential big ideas across lessons within a curriculum
V. Judicious Review Structured opportunities to recall or apply previously taught information	• Sufficient • Distributed over time • Cumulative • Varied • Judicious, not haphazard
VI. Primed Background Knowledge Preexisting information that affects new learning	• Aligns with learner knowledge and expertise • Considers strategic and proximal preskills • Readies learner for successful performance

in their book *Curriculum for a New Millennium,* it is estimated that by the late 1990s, the quantity of available information will double every 24 months. In effect, this means that learners in today's schools will be exposed to more information in a year than their grandparents were in a lifetime. For students who have difficulty acquiring and maintaining information, a focus on the most important ideas and concepts seems pivotal in managing the amount of information in textbooks.

The tendency of educators in the United States to expose students to a wealth of concepts and information without teaching them to understand or even put that information into a logical order is not new, and unfortunately it is not restricted to a particular subject area. Almost a decade ago, Porter (1989) discussed the consequences of curricula that teach for "exposure" and the impending compromises on depth of understanding. An article in *Education Week* also profiled the tendency of U.S. textbooks to emphasize breadth over depth:

> We cover lots and lots of things, more than anybody else in the world, but we don't do anything in great depth. . . . Science textbooks in the United States typically are two to four times longer than those in other countries . . . and yet it's just those constant snippets of information. While some countries expect 13 year olds to cover 10 to 15 scientific topics in depth, U.S. textbooks rush them through 30 or 40 topics. ("International Math and Science Study," 1994, p. 10)

Big ideas address the problem of the lack of depth in the curriculum. They are ideas, concepts, or principles that facilitate the most efficient and broadest acquisition of knowledge over the course of a particular subject (Carnine, 1994). By serving as anchoring concepts through which "small" ideas (more detailed information or additional facts) can often be understood, big ideas make it possible for students to learn as much as they can and learn it as efficiently as possible. For students with diverse learning needs, these conceptual anchors are increasingly important in this age of information proliferation.

The principal assumptions of big ideas are that (a) not all curriculum objectives and related instructional activities contribute equally to academic development and (b) more important information should be taught more thoroughly than less important information (Carnine, 1994). While some information is fundamental to a subject, other ideas simply are not essential, particularly for students with diverse learning needs who face the "tyranny of time" and must catch up with their peers (Kame'enui, 1993).

Big ideas should be the instructional anchors of programs for students with disabilities and diverse learning needs. This doesn't suggest that other information should not be taught, simply that it should not have equal weight with the basic, essential information or be given equal time. Although educators cannot make major overhauls in instructional materials, they can (a) identify big ideas and (b) evaluate lessons to determine the degree of adaptation necessary to ensure adequate instruction and practice of those big ideas.

Big Ideas Analysis

Approach

To determine the big ideas in a subject, educators must rely on two primary sources: (1) the curriculum content standards of their respective educational agency and (2) research-based areas of convergence. It is not teachers' responsibility to identify big ideas, but it is their duty to be thoroughly familiar with the skills, strategies, and knowledge that students are expected to demonstrate at specific grades. For example, in the area of beginning reading there are clear and consistent skills students should accomplish in their development of beginning reading (Committee on the Prevention of Reading Difficulties in Young Children, 1998). By the end of first grade, students should be able to segment three- to four-phoneme words auditorily, read three- to four-letter regular words accurately and fluently, answer literal comprehension questions, and retell simple stories including basic elements of story grammar. Once the big ideas or instructional priorities are identified, an analysis must be conducted of the alignment between learning expectations and the quality and quantity of instruction and practice in the instructional materials. Essentially, the focus of the analysis is this: Will the instruction and practice of the curricular materials result in students being able to demonstrate the target skill or strategy? To answer this question, select a representative lesson from a curricular program and consider the evaluative questions when evaluating or adapting curricular materials.

Analysis

In this section, we analyze objectives from a kindergarten language arts lesson. The content and instructional procedures focus on kindergarten concepts; however, we selected this lesson because the content and instruction are highly typical of what occurs not only in kindergarten lessons but also in basic concept lessons throughout the grades. In this and the other analyses that follow, we highlight the types of design and delivery problems that typify many popular programs. For copyright purposes, we cannot reproduce the lesson. We do, however, describe how to apply the evaluative questions to a particular lesson.

Lesson 1: Kindergarten Language Lesson

***Objectives* (as stated in the program):**

The lesson will enable each child to do the following:

1. Understand terms referring to size and use them correctly: *big, bigger, biggest, or large, larger, largest; little, littler, littlest, or small, smaller, smallest; same/different.*

2. Recognize likenesses and differences in size among members of a group.

Evaluative Questions

1. *Quantity of objectives: How many objectives are introduced in the lesson?*
   In this example lesson, a minimum of 12 objectives would be introduced because the introduction of each concept (e.g., *big, little, large, small*) constitutes a different objective.

2. *Coverage: Is the number of objectives reasonable for the full range of learners? Why or why not?*
   The number of objectives is *not reasonable* for students with learning difficulties because they are being asked to master a high number of different objectives. The fundamental concepts underlying big ideas are *priority, importance,* and *emphasis.* A basic problem is that the lesson introduces too many concepts with too little emphasis and development. Prior to and during the early stages of instruction, it is important to determine the knowledge that students bring to the learning context. It is prudent, however, to take the number of objectives at face value. If the program lists an objective (e.g., to understand terms referring to size, such as *big*), the objective should be treated as new information that is unfamiliar to students. For instance, consider the following nonsense concepts: *mif, ribble, merpe,* and *smult.* Each of these concepts could ostensibly represent a complex set of features, discriminations, and associated concepts. These nonsense concepts illustrate how introducing four new pieces of unfamiliar and conceptually similar information in one lesson can overwhelm students who have difficulty acquiring, retaining, and recalling basic and familiar information. As you work through this analysis, substitute the words *mif, ribble, merpe,* and *smult* for more familiar concepts to better understand the complexity of learning new concepts and the careful design needed for this kind of learning.
   Specific procedures to correct this problem will be discussed in the mediated scaffolding section of this analysis. A first step, however, is to reduce the number of objectives, or, in this case, new concepts intro-

TABLE 3
Identifying Big Ideas: Ranking Lesson Objectives

Ranking Lesson Objectives		
Lesson Objective	Is objective central and fundamental to later learning? (1–5 scale)	Is objective central and fundamental as an end goal? (1–5 scale)
Big/little	5	5
Large/small	a	a
Big/bigger/biggest	a	a

a = This objective is not a priority in this lesson, but would assume importance (i.e., it would rate a 5) in subsequent lessons.

duced in one lesson. There are two dimensions to consider when reducing the number of objectives in this lesson: (1) the number of new concepts (e.g., *big, little, large, small*) and (2) the concept of comparison (not introducing comparative and superlative concepts in the same lesson).

3. *Importance:* Using the format of Table 3, list the objectives in the lesson. Rate each objective according to importance using a 1–5 scale (1 = not very important; 5 = very important). Indicate whether each objective is central and fundamental to later learning or is central and fundamental as an end goal.

In this lesson, all the concepts introduced are important. The question is one of primacy and prior knowledge. If students do not know *big* or *little,* those concepts would be rated higher than *large* and *small* because *big* and *little* are typically more basic concepts. Ratings for *big* and *little* would be 5; *large* and *small* would still be important, but they would have a lower rating in early basic concept instruction. Likewise, the basic concepts of *big* and *little* are more fundamental than comparatives and superlatives.

4. *Time Priority:* Of the objectives you ranked as very important, how much priority/time will be allocated to them for instruction/practice within the lesson? Examine both teacher-directed and student-directed components of the lesson to determine the percentage of the lesson that will be allocated to the important objectives you determined.

TABLE 4
Identifying Big Ideas: Time Allocated to Objectives

Time Allocated to Objectives			
List content-priority objectives in the lesson	Percentage of time allocated to the objective *within* the lesson	Percentage of time allocated to the objective *across* subsequent lessons	Is the time allocated adequate for the full range of learners to be successful?[a]
Big	1	—	1
Little	1	—	1

[a]Scale: Highly adequate = 5; Somewhat adequate = 4; Adequate = 3; Somewhat inadequate = 2; Highly inadequate = 1

Next, examine the two subsequent lessons to determine the time allocated to the important objectives across lessons. Use both percentage-of-time columns in Table 4 to determine whether the time allocated to the objective is adequate for the *full range of learners* to be successful.

5. *Objectives:* How many objectives within the lessons you are analyzing align with the objectives/goals you have prioritized above? Examine the individual lessons and calculate the objectives (by percent) *within* the lessons that align with prioritized objectives (Table 5). Based on your analysis, identify the modifications necessary to accommodate the full range of learners. Select all that apply:

- Decrease the number of objectives within a lesson.
- Allocate more time to content-priority objectives within a lesson. Specify which and how.
- Allocate more time to content-priority objectives across lessons. Specify which and how.
- Increase percentage of objectives aligned with state-prioritized objectives.

TABLE 5
Identifying Big Ideas:
Percentage of Objectives That Align with Prioritized Goals

Percentage of Lesson Objectives Aligned with Prioritized Goals	
Lesson #	Percentage of Objectives to Prioritized Goals

II. Conspicuous Strategies

The second step in the analysis assesses the quality of instruction and whether the instructional recommendations will communicate the complex, cognitive information to the learner effectively and efficiently. Step II involves assessing whether instruction is conspicuous. That is, does it communicate clearly and explicitly the steps the learner must employ to perform the strategy and complete the task?

To solve problems, students follow a set of steps or strategies. Many students develop their own strategies, but a considerable amount of time may be required for the student to identify the optimum strategy. For students with disabilities and diverse learning needs, such an approach is highly problematic because instructional time is a precious commodity and these learners may never figure out an effective or efficient strategy. Learning is most efficient when a teacher can make it conspicuous or explicit. In addition, strategies are most effective when they are of medium breadth and generalizable.

When applied to a process such as reading comprehension or to a specific skill such as determining the main idea in a paragraph or a story, a conspicuous strategy is the set of steps that leads students to comprehend and identify the main idea effectively and efficiently. Unfortunately, many students with diverse learning needs are unable to intuit or figure out the relationship of the main idea to the whole paragraph or story before the opportunities for learning have been exhausted. Moreover, the curriculum may not provide the strategic steps necessary for teachers to communicate the process adequately.

Teachers, then, must devise ways to make clear to the students the strategies proficient readers use to

- determine whether the main idea is explicitly or implicitly stated,
- discriminate most important from less important information,
- summarize ideas, and
- come to a reasonable conclusion.

Conspicuous Strategies Analysis

A strategy is a series of steps students use to achieve a goal. In instruction, it is important that these steps initially be made overt and conspicuous for students. As students learn a strategy, the steps should become more covert.

To determine whether curricular materials will need to be adapted, continue with the same lesson used for the Big Ideas analysis. Use the evaluative questions to assess the conspicuousness of the instructional strategies.

Excerpt of Instructional Language

Display a picture of a family at a farm (i.e., the picture depicts four or five family members interacting with many farm animals of varying sizes). Explain that the class will compare the size of different things. Call attention to the horse and to the dog beside it. Say: "The horse is big in size. Another word for *big* is *large*. The dog is little in size. Another word for *little* is *small*. Point to other things in the picture that are big. Point to other things in the picture that are little." Call on volunteers to answer each question, and have each volunteer tell whether the thing he or she is pointing to is big or little.

Evaluative Questions

Find the directions for one of the important objectives selected in the Big Idea analysis and answer the following questions:

1. *Do the directions require the teacher to (check the one that applies)*
   - *Model the skill/strategy? (Demonstrate before asking students to apply the strategy.)*
   - *Explain the skill/strategy? (Describe.)*
   - *Reference/note the skill/strategy?*
   - *Other?*

Example choice: *Model the skill/strategy.* In this lesson, the instructions ask the teacher to model/show the learner one example of each concept ("The horse is big in size").

2. *Is the instruction sufficiently conspicuous to enable the full range of learners to demonstrate/perform the skill? (Yes/No/Maybe)*

Example choice: *Maybe.* Although the teacher did tell the learner "the horse is big and the dog is little," many problems remain, but they stem largely from the limited number of modeled examples. (*Note:* The solution to this problem will also be discussed in the mediated scaffolding section.)

3. *Are the directions clear and sufficient for you to know how to teach the skill? (Yes/No/Maybe)*

Example choice: *Yes* (although the instruction is problematic in other areas). The instructional language in this lesson is fairly good and commendable. The initial language used to model and communicate information was clear and easy for students to understand (e.g., "This horse is big").

4. *Is the strategy useful, and will it lead to efficient/generalizable learning for the full range of learning? (Yes/No/Maybe)*

Example choice: *Probably not.* Students with learning difficulties will need more modeling of more carefully controlled examples to learn the strategy well enough to transfer it to other examples. Presenting only one example of "big" and one example of "little" is simply not enough, and it will not lead to generalizable learning. (See next section.)

5. *Does the lesson apply the strategy to many examples of the target skill (objective)? Based on your analysis, identify the modifications necessary to accommodate the full range of learners (select all that apply):*

- *Change or add a strategy.*
- *Modify language/teaching to make more explicit.*
- *Add examples to which the strategy applies.*

Example choice: *Add examples to which the strategy applies.*

III. Mediated Scaffolding

In Step III, the analysis focuses on the instructional support or scaffolding that enhances cognitive access. Generally, scaffolding is the help or guidance teachers give students as they acquire new knowledge. As such, it may be the most intuitive of the six guidelines discussed in this book, particularly with respect to students with learning difficulties. In cognitive scaffolding, the goal is for students to "get it," or understand the first step in the learning process. The role of the scaffolding, however, is to eliminate the problems that could block students from getting it: not understanding or remembering the sound-meaning correspondence in learning to read, for example, or developing a dislike for the activity and giving up.

Additionally, the scaffolding is temporary. Students acquiring knowledge should learn to become as self-regulated and independent as possible. To accomplish this, teachers should gradually remove the scaffolding. On new or difficult tasks, scaffolding may be substantial at first and then be systematically removed as learners acquire knowledge and skills. For example, scaffolding can be accomplished through multiple formats, including the careful selection of examples that progress from less difficult to more difficult, the purposeful separation of highly similar and potentially confusing facts and concepts (e.g., mitosis and meiosis; /p/ and /b/ in early letter–sound correspondence learning), the strategic sequencing of tasks that require learners to recognize and then produce a response, or the additional information that selected examples provide, such as highlighting the digits used in a division problem.

This type of guidance can be critical for students with diverse learning needs, yet recent studies indicate that it is lacking in U.S. textbooks, as compared to the instructional tools of other nations. Specifically, Mayer, Sims, and Tajika's (1995) comparison of how American and Japanese textbooks teach mathematical problem solving indicated that "Japanese textbooks contained many more worked-out examples . . . than did the U.S. books" (p. 457). One of the primary conclusions was that the Japanese textbooks tend to support learners in the learning process through multiple examples of successful problem-solving strategies, whereas "in the U.S., textbooks are more likely to provide lots of exercises for students to solve on their own without much guidance" (p. 457).

Scaffolding is not a static, predetermined instructional condition. The degree of scaffolding changes with the abilities of the learner, the goals of instruction, and the complexities of the task. Educators must determine the level and degree of scaffolding necessary. Nonetheless, the more built-in support structures contained in curricular materials, the easier it is for teachers to provide the scaffolding that learners require.

The scaffolding analysis that follows addresses the following question: Do the amount, sequence, and selection of information enhance the probability that information will be learned?

Mediated Scaffolding Analysis

Mediated scaffolding is the support/guidance provided to students in the form of steps, tasks, materials, and personal support during initial learning. As the learner progresses toward self-directed learning, the external supports are withdrawn. Some refer to scaffolds as *prompts* or *guides*.

Evaluative Questions

To assess the quality of scaffolding, answer the following questions. (The answers to these questions refer to the lesson excerpt found in the "Conspicuous Strategies" section [p. 16]).

1. *Does the sequence of instruction move from teacher-directed to student-directed activities?*
    Yes, although only one example of each concept is presented.

2. *Does the sequence of instruction provide multiple examples of the target strategy prior to asking the learner to perform the skill?*
    No, only one example of *big* is provided; only one example of *little* is modeled prior to asking students to apply the concept to other examples.
    Another problem is that the examples used to illustrate the concepts are inadequate. "The horse is big; the dog is little." There are many factors that are different about a horse and a dog that learners could confuse, such as color, actions, position in space, and so on. If the horse is brown and the dog is white, that could possibly be the factor children identify as the differentiation between big and little. Teachers must take care to ensure that curriculum examples control the irrelevant features so that learners focus on the most salient feature of a concept. A way to remedy this problem is to use only pictures of *dogs* (i.e., a big dog and a little dog, both of which are the same in every way except size). The language would be the same for both except for the critical feature—size.

3. *Does the sequence begin with easy tasks and progress to more difficult ones?*
    Yes; however, the progression is very quick. The instruction moves from one example of the concept *big* to a synonym *large*, then introduces yet another example of a new concept, *little*, as well as its synonym *small*. This fast rate and lack of emphasis are likely to present problems for students who need more carefully designed instruction.

---

4. *Does the sequence of instruction separate potentially confusing information? Does the lesson introduce concepts or ideas that the learner may confuse?*

This is one of the most problematic areas of this lesson. In a single lesson, the instruction introduces two similar concepts (i.e., *big*, *little*), their respective synonyms, and then comparatives and superlatives of those concepts. A better design would be to introduce only one concept (i.e., *big*) and provide many examples of things that are big and things that are not big prior to introducing the concept and label *little*. Moreover, the term *large* should not be introduced until students are firm on the concept of *big*.

5. *Does the sequence introduce a manageable amount of information for the range of learners?*

No. Far too much information is introduced. The concepts should be introduced and taught in several lessons.

6. *Count the number of modeled examples prior to learner practice.*

There is one modeled example.

7. *Count the number of guided examples prior to independent work.*

The number of guided examples cannot be determined here. Because the teacher calls on volunteers, it is impossible to determine the number of guided practice opportunities students will have. What is obvious is that calling only on volunteers is not likely to give the teacher a good idea of how well children with diverse learning needs understand the concept of *big* or *little*.

8. *Do the requirements in instruction parallel requirements in independent practice? Examine the teaching component of the lesson and compare it with the expectations of practice/independent work. Based on your analysis, identify the modifications necessary to accommodate the full range of learners:*

- Add explicit models designed by the teacher prior to student application.
- Add more examples of the skill/strategy in the guided practice phase.
- Reduce the amount of information in the lesson.
- Separate potentially confusing information/skills.
- Sequence tasks to progress from easy to more difficult.
- Change independent activities to parallel instructional activities.

IV. Strategic Integration

For new information to be understood and applied, it should be carefully combined (strategically integrated) with what the learner already knows and understands to produce a more generalizable, higher-order skill. Integrating new information with existing knowledge increases the likelihood that new information will be understood at a deeper level. But it must be done strategically and the critical connections made clear so that the new information does not become confused with what the learner already knows. For example, in teaching students how to compose narratives, a teacher can move from activities based on reading comprehension, such as identification and application of narrative elements (e.g., setting, main characters, initiating event, resolution to the problem), to generation of those elements. Similarly, in beginning reading, once learners can hear sounds in words and recognize letter–sound correspondences fluently, those skills can be integrated to recognize words. These powerful and oftentimes logical connections comprise strategic integration.

Integrated curricula are currently popular. However, as the following analogy illustrates, the term *integration* can be used somewhat ambiguously. Most people are familiar with the elementary chemistry concept of combining (or integrating) materials to form either mixtures or new compounds. In mixtures, materials retain their original properties, while in compounds, properties change and something new emerges.

Strategic integration is the carefully controlled combination of what the student already knows with what he or she has to learn so that the relationship between these two elements is clear and results in new or more complete knowledge.

Examples of strategic integration include:

- Using text structure to enhance reading comprehension and then as a basis for narrative writing.

- Integrating letter–sound correspondence knowledge to form words.

- Using the strategy for solving proportions as a basis for word problem solving.

In an integrated curriculum, there is no particular advantage to mixing knowledge or learning facts across subject areas for the simple sake of mixing. In fact, students may try to make connections that do not exist. In contrast, however, there is tremendous potential benefit in compounding knowledge—that is, integrating information across subject areas to show the important interrelationships so that new, more complete knowledge structures result. Additionally, many potentially confusing concepts can be preempted or corrected through the careful integration of knowledge.

Strategic Integration Analysis

Select a highly important skill/strategy identified in your earlier analysis. Examine subsequent lessons to answer the following questions. (The answers that follow are based on the same curriculum excerpt as in the previous section.)

Evaluative Questions

1. *Does the lesson make explicit the connections between prior learning and new skills?*

No. However, because these are new concepts, it may not be necessary to connect them to previously taught information. When working with basic concepts such as *big* and *little*, children have few previous connections. If the instruction had introduced *big* and *little* in previous lessons and *large* and *small* were newly introduced concepts, then the strategic connection with known concepts would be highly appropriate and important.

2. *Where appropriate, does the lesson explain the relationship among its components/parts?*

Yes. This is an excerpt from a lesson, so it is difficult to see the complete progression of activities in which the new concepts are applied. In the excerpt, there is a connection between the teacher-modeled examples and student-generated examples.

3. *Does the lesson result in the learner being able to demonstrate a higher-order concept/strategy based on integration of prior learning and new learning?*

No, not as currently designed. This lesson did not sufficiently develop the core concept or building block (i.e., *big*) necessary to develop more complex skills. The correct design would develop solid understanding of one concept, such as *big*, and systematically build on that knowledge in subsequent lessons to develop understanding of the relation of *big*, *bigger*, and *biggest*, which would allow learners to make higher-order connections. Higher-order concepts depend, however, on understanding of foundational concepts such as *big* or *small*. To rush into teaching comparative and superlative concepts when children do not know basic concepts will compromise later and more complex learning.

4. *Identify the modifications necessary to accommodate the full range of learners.*

- Make explicit the connections between prior learning and new learning.
- Make explicit the connections between the components within a lesson.
- Indicate how the new objective results in a higher-order skill or strategy.

V. Judicious Review

Successful learning also depends on a review process to reinforce the essential building blocks of information within a subject area. But simple repetition of information does not necessarily ensure efficient learning; it must be carefully considered.

Dixon, Carnine, and Kame'enui (1992) identified four critical dimensions of judicious review:

1. It should be sufficient to enable a student to perform a task without hesitation.

2. It should be distributed over time.

3. It should be cumulative, and the information should be integrated into more complex tasks.

4. It should be varied to illustrate the wide application of a student's understanding of the information.

So how does a teacher select information for review, schedule review to ensure retention, and design activities to extend a learner's understanding of the skills, concepts, or strategies?

According to Dempster (1991), "spaced repetitions," in which a learner is asked to recall a learning experience, are more effective than "massed repetition," if the "spacing between occurrences is relatively short" (p. 73). As early as 1917, Edward (cited in Dempster, 1991) observed that elementary school children who studied academic information once for 4 minutes and again for 2½ minutes several days later retained about 30% more information than students receiving one continuous 6½-minute session. Repeated presentations of shorter time increments distributed over time should, therefore, be considered when scheduling instruction.

Judicious Review Analysis

To develop retention, students must be given opportunities to practice and review skills and strategies. Minimally, these review opportunities must be sufficiently frequent to facilitate automatic application of the skill/strategy and sufficiently distributed to ensure that students retain the skill/strategy over time.

Analyze the lesson in which the objective is initially introduced plus the next three to four lessons.

Evaluative Questions

1. *Is there adequate review of the new skill/strategy within the introductory lesson?*

No. Neither the amount nor the type of review is adequate in the introductory lesson. A basic reason why there is insufficient review revolves around the problem of establishing clear priorities. Because there are many concepts introduced in one lesson, this lessens the amount of review any single concept will receive. In addition, using volunteers to answer questions about *big* and *little* will not allow teachers to determine whether all students know the concept of *big*.

2. *Examine the next three lessons and document the lessons in which the information from the current lesson is reviewed or included as part of instruction or practice.*

The skill/strategy was reviewed/applied the following number of times in:

1. The adjacent lesson.

2. The next two lessons.

3. The next three lessons.

4. Other (please specify).

3. *Analyze the skill/strategy horizontally; that is, identify the lesson in which the skill is initially introduced and the lesson schedule in which it is reviewed. Record the lesson number in the table on page 25.*

The essence of judicious review is that new information and associated tasks are reviewed regularly and systematically. (Criteria 2 and 3 cannot be analyzed here because our excerpt is from a single lesson.) To conduct this analysis, examine the current lesson and a minimum of three to four subsequent lessons to determine whether the concept is reviewed, practiced, and applied in different tasks and contexts. Typically, there is very little systematic review across lessons. This

Objective/Skill	Lesson Number in Which Objective Is Reviewed			
	1	2	3	4
Objective #1:				
Objective #2:				
Objective #3:				

poses serious difficulties for students who have difficulty retaining new and unfamiliar information.

VI. Primed Background Knowledge

Successful acquisition of new information depends largely on (a) the knowledge the learner brings to a task, (b) the accuracy of that information, and (c) the degree to which the learner accesses and uses that information. For students with disabilities and diverse learning needs, priming background knowledge is critical to success because it addresses the memory and strategy deficits they bring to certain tasks. In effect, priming is a brief reminder or prompt that alerts the learner to task dimensions or to retrieve known information.

Instructional materials can acknowledge the importance of background knowledge in two ways. First, students can be pretested for important background knowledge. Such tests can be used to determine placement within an instructional program or to alert teachers to the need for allocating time to background topics. It is often useful to assess the background knowledge of students with learning difficulties using formats other than reading and writing because these students frequently understand more than they can express through reading or writing.

Second, instructional programs can include important background knowledge in the scope of topics taught. Ideally, such background topics would be taught or reviewed a few days before the introduction of new strategies that depend upon those topics. If background topics are introduced earlier than that, students may forget some relevant aspects by the time the new strategy is introduced. If background topics are introduced in the same lesson as the new strategy, some students are likely to be overwhelmed by the quantity of new knowledge.

Clearly, the concept of strategic integration is closely related to essential background knowledge. The focus on strategic integration, however, emphasized increasing depth of understanding of important concepts. Here, the focus is on the prerequisites for learning important concepts so that they might be integrated meaningfully.

Primed Background Knowledge Analysis

Background knowledge has multiple dimensions. When analyzing lessons, it is important to discriminate *language* background knowledge from *component* background knowledge. *Language background knowledge* refers to knowledge the learner has of the vocabulary and concepts used in a task. This type of knowledge is most critical to comprehension. *Component background knowledge* refers to the prerequisite component skills necessary to perform a new task.

Continue the analysis with the selected lesson (here, the previously selected excerpt).

Evaluative Questions

1. *Identify the language background knowledge required of the task.*

 • *Does the lesson adequately explain or access this knowledge?*

2. *Identify the component background knowledge required of the task.*

 • *Does the lesson adequately explain or access this knowledge?*

3. *Identify the modifications necessary to accommodate the full range of learners.*

 • *Identify and access knowledge of language that is prerequisite to the objective.*

 • *Identify and access knowledge of components that are prerequisites to the objective.*

Because this is a language lesson, the language and the components might appear in another curricular domain (e.g., reading, social studies, math). Nonetheless, the instructions of this lesson required children to "compare the size of different things." The lesson also introduced basic concepts such as *big* and *little*. Teachers must attend to the instructional language used, such as "compare" and "different," to ensure that the learning is not short-circuited by the words used in instructions. It is highly likely that students who do not understand the concepts *big* or *little* also may not understand *different* and *compare*.

This is an introductory lesson for *big* and *little;* therefore, there is little prior component language students would require to be able to perform the tasks successfully.

Summary of Analysis of the Six Principles of Effective Curriculum Design

I. Big Ideas: Limit the number of new concepts introduced in a lesson, and focus first on the most basic concepts before advancing to the more complex concepts. Introduce *big* or *little,* not both in one lesson, and be sure that students understand one concept before introducing the second. Reserve teaching synonyms until students are firm on the basic concept. The concepts of comparatives and superlatives should be withheld until the basic concepts are clearly established. When introducing comparatives and superlatives, introduce comparatives first; then, after students consistently use comparatives, introduce superlatives.

II. Conspicuous Strategies: Use clear models, as this lesson did, to teach basic concepts. The simplicity of the language in this lesson was appropriate; it did not try to complicate a simple concept by using other, unnecessary language. The basic limitation of this lesson was that it used a limited number of examples to model the target concepts prior to asking students to apply their knowledge of *big* and *little.*

III. Mediated Scaffolding: Limit the number of concepts introduced, and separate those that are likely to be confused. Remember that while *mif* and *ribble* may represent common concepts to us, they might seem to be nonsense to the learner. To reduce the language demands, refrain from introducing two new and unfamiliar labels in one day. Instead of introducing a new label (e.g., *ribble*), it is easier to refer to the other concept as "not mif." It is also important to provide sufficient guided practice for the group before progressing to individual turns.

IV. Strategic Integration: When the basic concept of *big* is reliably known by learners, then introduce comparative and superlative concepts strategically to build higher-order skills. Higher-order skills will not be useful or reliable if the basic concepts are not firm.

V. *Judicious Review:* To really "know" a concept, students must use it frequently and in a variety of contexts. Lessons following the initial lesson should apply new concepts to build up the students' ability to remember and recall the concepts.

VI. *Primed Background Knowledge:* A frequent limitation of early language programs is using language that learners may not understand. If the objective of the lesson is to introduce the concepts *big* and *little,* then directions that tell children we will "compare" objects may not be meaningful. Examine the instructional language carefully to determine whether it will need to be simplified. It is also important to ensure that students have the prerequisite knowledge (e.g., understanding of *mibble*) before using that knowledge in more complex contexts (e.g., *mibbler, mibblest*).

4

Application of Instructional Design Principles to Beginning Reading and Expository Writing

The following applications of the six principles in the areas of reading and writing exemplify the curriculum design that is both possible of and necessary for high-quality tools for the full range of learners. Although the big ideas across the various subject areas are necessarily different, the principles for how and when to teach those ideas are similar. That is, understanding mediated scaffolding, primed background knowledge, strategic integration, conspicuous strategies, and judicious review in the context of teaching phonological awareness in beginning reading helps you use these same strategies in the context of teaching concepts in other content areas, including history, mathematics, writing, and so on. In the following examples, we illustrate how the curriculum design principles relate to content in beginning reading and writing.

Beginning Reading

Big Idea: Phonological Awareness

Recent research in reading (Smith, Simmons, & Kame'enui, 1995) concluded that beginning readers must be able to hear and manipulate sounds in words and understand the sound structure of language. Evidence derived from dozens of primary and secondary sources confirmed that children who are strong in phonological awareness usually learn to read more easily than children who are weak in this skill

(Juel, 1998; Smith, Gleason, Kame'enui, & Baker, in press; Stanovich, 1986; Torgesen, Wagner, & Rashotte, 1994). Evidence further indicates that phonological awareness is (a) a complex process composed of many components, (b) a reliable predictor for later reading achievement, (c) causally related to reading development, and (d) successfully developed through instruction and practice. From this, one can ascertain that the ability to hear and manipulate sounds in language is a big idea and is key to early reading acquisition.

In beginning reading, big ideas are those unifying curricular activities that enable learners to translate the alphabetic code into meaningful language. Because these skills are fundamental to beginning reading, they deserve considerable focus and attention in the early reading curriculum. Big ideas can also provide guidelines about the essential components of beginning reading programs.

Representative Example

The following example is representative of the types of activities first-grade basal reading programs use to promote phonological awareness. According to the teacher's guide, the objective of the following activity is to develop phonemic awareness of /s/. The strategy requires learners to identify the sound of the letter at the beginning of *sun* and *sister* and compare other words to determine whether the initial sound is a match to the initial sound of the target words. In essence, the task requires learners to make a word-to-word match based on the similarity of initial sounds. This example provides nine words from which students discriminate those that begin with the same sound as *sun* and *sister* and those that do not. Figure 1 shows the task as presented in the teacher's guide.

The example requires students to sort through several sentences to discern the objective of the task—that is, to determine that /s/ is the target sound. The success of this task is also predicated on learners' understanding of the concept *beginning* and their ability to extract the desired objective from two example target words. The complexity of the task is further complicated by requiring students to discriminate between words that begin the same as *sun* and *sister* and those that do not.

We reiterate that this instruction may be sufficient for some learners in first grade; nevertheless, many children will require more careful attention to the architecture of instruction. The following modifications may seem commonplace and straightforward, but recent research indicates that they are not characteristic of either traditional or nontraditional basal reading programs in general education.

FIGURE 1
Representative Activity from Existing Basal Reading Program

Big Idea: Phonological Awareness

---

1. Existing Example

Teach/Model

INCONSPICUOUS STRATEGY: Word-to-Word Matching

Develop phonemic awareness of /s/.

Tell children they will be learning about the letter that stands for the sound they hear at the beginning of *sun*. Have children stand. Have them repeat the words *sun* and *sister.* Tell them you will say some words. Have them repeat each word and then squat each time they hear a word that begins the same as *sun* and *sister: safe, say, not, sell, mend, gate, send, seed, dip.*

---

2. Enhanced Example

Teach/Model

CONSPICUOUS STRATEGY: Sound Isolation

Teacher (Models /s/ sound.) "Today we will be learning about the sound you hear at the beginning of *sun.* The beginning sound in *sun* is /s/. Listen as I say the beginning sound in words: sun, /s/; sister, /s/; safe, /s/; say, /s/; sell /s/."

Students (Listen to the words and their beginning sound.)

Teacher (Assists student understanding of sound isolation.) "When I say a word, you say the beginning sound and then the word: *sun, seed, send, sit, surf.*"

Students (Isolate beginning /s/ in words.)

Teacher (Assesses student understanding of sound isolation.) "Now I'll say some words that begin with /s/ and some that begin with other sounds you have learned. When I say a word, you tell me the beginning sound and then say the word: *sun, sand, tame, sip, seed, get, send, not, lamp, sell.*"

Students (Isolate beginning /s/ and other sounds in words.)

---

continues

FIGURE 1 *(Continued)*

3. Mediated Scaffolding Example

Teach/Model

CONSPICUOUS STRATEGY: Word Segmentation	
Teacher	(Models segmenting words that begin with /s/.) "Now we are going to say all the sounds in words. Listen as I say the sounds in words: *sun* /s/ /u/ /n/; *sat* /s/ /a/ /t/; *sip* /s/ /i/ /p/; *send* /s/ /e/ /n/ /d/."
Students	(Listen to sounds in words that begin with /s/.)
Teacher	(Assists student understanding of segmenting words that begin with /s/.) "When I say a word, you tell me the sounds in the word: *sun, sad, sit, sell, sob.*"
Students	(Segment words that begin with /s/.)
Teacher	(Assists student understanding of segmenting words that begin with /s/ and other sounds.) "Now I will say some words that begin with /s/ and some words that do not begin with /s/. When I say a word, you tell me the sounds in the word: *sun, sad, hot, sit, sell, bin, man, sob, let, sat.*"
Students	(Segment words that begin with /s/ and other sounds.)

Enhanced Example

The activity in the existing example may pose problems for a range of learners in general education. But these problems can be corrected through attending to the curriculum design principles of conspicuous strategies and mediated scaffolding.

Conspicuous strategies in beginning reading are the steps that lead to effective and efficient word recognition. In phonological awareness, they are the steps a reader takes to learn the sound structure of a word. Unfortunately, many learners do not intuit and cannot figure out the processes of blending or segmenting sounds in words before losing much ground. As seen in the enhanced example, a teacher can help the students better understand the sounds by making explicit the steps used to manipulate those sounds internally and by working through the parts that need to be conspicuous for them.

The teacher models the information, first introducing easier tasks, and then provides practice with multiple examples of similar activities during which students may notice the commonalities in the target words and observe task expectation. These activities are provided prior to requiring discrimination exercises. Through this sequence of teaching events and teacher actions, the instructional strategies requirements of the task are made more explicit.

In addition to conspicuous strategies, the enhanced example uses several forms of *mediated scaffolding*, which refers to the external support provided by teacher, tasks, and materials during initial learning of sounds, letters, and words. First, teachers model the process of matching initial sounds of words. Next, initial learning is supported by focusing first on words with /s/. Before students are asked to discriminate words that begin with /s/ from those that do not, they practice identifying the initial sound in words that begin with /s/. Discrimination words (e.g., *not, gate*) are introduced only after students have had multiple opportunities to hear the critical feature (the initial /s/ sound) of words.

In the existing example, instruction and practice focused largely on detecting and matching sounds in the initial positions of words. Although this is a logical first step in a task continuum, the focus can expand through mediated scaffolding to having students identify and manipulate sounds in all positions of words.

Up to this point, the enhanced example has not differed radically from the original activity, although the outcomes are likely to be more promising. The alterations of teacher modeling, additional examples, control of the learning set, and gradual movement to discrimination exercises all can be achieved with modest modification. In a final enhancement, a new phonological awareness activity can be added to increase both the complexity and the level of alteration—a word segmentation component.

The goal of incorporating word segmentation exercises is to structure practice on those progressively more difficult phonological awareness processes—those processes that approximate the auditory requirements of word reading. In this alteration, it is important to scaffold this new activity in multiple ways. First, simpler phonological awareness tasks are introduced and practiced several lessons prior to introducing the more complex task. Second, word segmenting is modeled and practiced with words that begin with /s/ and then extended to words with other sounds already introduced in the program.

Written Expression

Big Ideas

The way a text is structured establishes relationships between ideas through recognition of well-organized patterns and understanding of how text structure can be applied in teaching reading comprehension and composition. Specifically, the principle of comparing and contrasting text structures is a big idea because it establishes interrelationships between topics (e.g., Native Americans in the Northwest and in the Great Plains) and features (e.g., how food, housing, and transportation are related). By using a compare/contrast organization, students can identify and learn key concepts and networks of information. Furthermore, knowledge or awareness of how to compare and contrast text structure can be used in various content areas, reading comprehension tasks, and written composition.

Focusing on a particular text structure is a first step in instruction. Subsequent instructional decisions must address how to teach the text structure efficiently and effectively. Table 6 illustrates the five remaining instructional design principles and their relations when teaching the big idea compare/contrast text structure. In this table, the instructional guidelines are presented separately in columns for clarity. However, in actual lesson plans they should be thoughtfully interwoven to frame effective instruction for students with disabilities.

Conspicuous Strategies

The procedures for teaching conspicuous strategies using applications from compare/contrast text structure are detailed below.

1. *Inform students when and why the strategy is helpful.*

   - *Specific application:* Using compare/contrast text structure will help you summarize important information.

   - *Example:* When you read the passage on the four groups of Native Americans who inhabited Canada, use the compare/contrast components to help identify features and organize similarities and differences.

2. *Define and explain the strategy components.*

   - *Specific application:* The components of compare/contrast text structure are (a) an introduction that tells what is compared/contrasted, (b) similarities, (c) differences, (d) key words, and (e) conclusion.

   - *Example:* The first paragraph is an introduction. It tells the reader what is being compared/contrasted and the features of comparison.

TABLE 6
Examples of Interweaving the Five Instructional Design Principles Across Lessons Involving the Components of Compare/Contrast Text Structure

Conspicuous Strategy	Mediated Scaffolding	Strategic Integration	Primed Background Knowledge	Judicious Review
Tell when and why compare/contrast text structure is helpful		Apply to school and practical tasks	Discuss before introducing new task	Review systematically before and after new tasks
Define and explain components	Use explicit text to model identifying components	Use authentic text to model and explain components	Require students to recall components before reading compare/contrast information	Apply to more difficult tasks such as composition or editing
Model strategy	Model use to identify important information	Apply to a composition strategy	Require students to recall procedures before composing	Teach peers to model strategy
Teach self-verbalization	Think aloud during modeling	Require students to verbalize strategy steps while writing a rough draft	Require students to verbalize components before writing a rough draft	Incorporate features in peer editing
Provide feedback	Model how to provide feedback to self; model how peers provide feedback to each other	Provide feedback on students' compare/contrast notesheet	Require students to self-edit a rough draft	Require peer editing

3. *Model the strategy.*

- *Specific application:* Model how to locate compare/contrast information in students' textbook.

- *Example:* "I do not see an introductory paragraph telling the topics of compare/contrast, so I need to read to find the information. The dark subheadings tell me the first section is about the Northwest and Plains Native Americans. I write `Northwest' and `Plains Native Americans' on the lines for topics on my notesheet. You do the same on your notesheets. Next, I read to find the compare/contrast features. The first feature the section on Northwest Native Americans tells about is the type of houses they lived in. I will write `houses' under `Feature' on the notesheet and describe their houses in the box for that information. You do the same."

4. *Teach students to self-verbalize the strategy.*

- *Specific application:* Require students to memorize the steps for identifying and summarizing important compare/contrast information (i.e., identify topics, identify features, record the features on a notesheet, decide whether the features are similarities or differences, reorganize the features in parallel format, draft a summary, edit, revise).

- *Example:* "You recorded the features of compare/contrast. What do you do next?"

5. *Provide feedback at key points in the learning process.*

- *Specific application:* Provide feedback to students on the quality of their conclusions to their summaries.

- *Example:* Call on volunteers to read their conclusions. Call on other volunteers to tell what is good about the conclusions and what needs to be improved. The teacher may also provide input. After several examples of conclusions, provide students an opportunity to revise their own conclusions.

Mediated Scaffolding

In teaching expository text structure, the concept of mediated scaffolding involves three features:

1. Modeling by teacher and peers.
2. Sequencing content and tasks to move from easier to more difficult.

3. Using systematically designed materials to guide students as they learn and apply strategies (Dickson, Simmons, & Kame'enui, 1998).

Teacher scaffolding for instruction of compare/contrast text structure occurred primarily through teacher modeling. When modeling compare/contrast components in well- or poorly written passages, teachers verbalized their thought processes. For example, the teachers said, "I recorded information about the houses of the Woodland Native Americans, so I need to look for information about the houses of the Plains groups." "Their houses are different, so I will use the arrow that shows differences." "Here is an *-er* word, so I will look for a comparison."

Following teacher models, *peers* modeled the process for each other. The class was divided into two groups, high- and low-performing students. Each low-performing student was matched with a high-performing student. The pairs performed each step of the identification process together, with the high-performing students modeling the process for low-performing students. Each member of the pair recorded the information on his or her own notesheet.

Task scaffolding occurred as teachers gradually increased the level of difficulty of the tasks. For example, when introducing the components of compare/contrast structure, teachers first used explicit passages adapted from the social studies textbook (i.e., passages that contained easily identifiable components and key words) for initial modeling and practice. Second, teachers used passages with missing components, having students identify and supply the missing components. Next, students applied the strategy to passages in their textbooks. They compared and contrasted information in the textbook (e.g., how French and English settlers of Canada relate to people with French or English backgrounds in Canada today; the differences in settling the eastern and western parts of Canada; how industry in Canada and the United States compares). Finally, students used the compare/contrast components to compose well-organized summaries of social studies topics (e.g., French and English settlers in Canada).

Material scaffolding occurred through the use of strategically sequenced materials. For example, in one compare/contrast study (Dickson, 1994), highly prompted materials were used in each phase of initial learning and were strategically sequenced to guide students' comprehension and composition.

First, students used notesheets to learn to identify compare/contrast information in their textbooks (Figure 2). They used the same notesheets to determine whether the features were similar or different (also Figure 2). An organization sheet guided their rearrangement of information in preparation for summary writing (Figure 3). A prompt-

FIGURE 2
Compare/Contrast Notesheet
for Identifying Topics and Features and Determining
Whether Features Are Differences or Similarities

Compare/Contrast Notesheet

Key Words: -er words, *different, but, like, similarly, in contrast*

Questions to ask:
1. What is being compared?
2. What features are being compared?
3. How are they alike?
4. How are they different?

Theme:

Use this arrow ⟶ to tell whether features are alike.
Use this arrow ⟶ to tell whether features are different.
Use a question mark (?) if you cannot tell.

Feature	A	Alike or Different	B

---

ed rough draft sheet (Figure 4) reminded students to include an introduction, key words, and a conclusion in addition to similarities and
differences. Finally, an edit sheet (Figure 5) reminded students to check
the inclusion of an introduction, similarities, differences, key words,
and a conclusion. The edit sheet also provided editors and authors
with an opportunity to comment on what was well written in the summary.

In summary, scaffolding should be adjusted to students' needs and
faded as students gain proficiency in each phase of instruction. Initial

FIGURE 3
Compare/Contrast Organization Sheet for
Providing a Framework for Bipolar or
Integrated Parallel Construction of a Composition

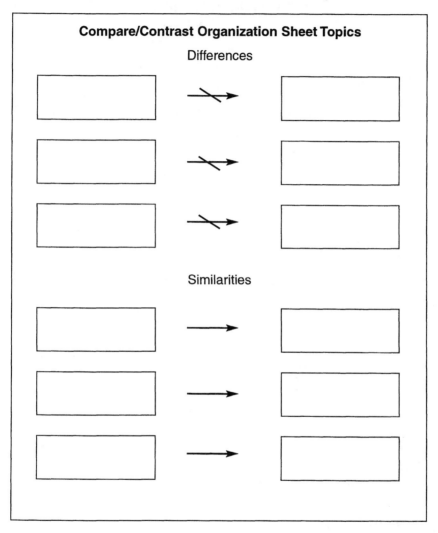

instruction in each phase of learning included teacher modeling, easy content and tasks (e.g., identifying compare/contrast elements), and highly prompted materials. Following initial instruction in each phase (e.g., identifying compare/contrast components, transposing compare/contrast information to notesheets, writing summaries), students

FIGURE 4
Prompted Compare/Contrast Rough Draft Sheet

Rough Draft (Prompted) Compare/Contrast		
Introduction • Tells theme • Tells topic Conclusion	Similarities Differences Supporting Details	Comparison Words • -er • different • like • similarly • but • in contrast

progressed toward independent work as teacher scaffolding faded to peer scaffolding and content and tasks became more complex. Additionally, lower-performing students maintained access to the highly prompted support materials.

Strategic Integration

One of the pervasive problems faced by students with learning disabilities is their failure to generalize learning to new tasks and content. To promote generalization, instruction should use authentic, realistic tasks to demonstrate the usefulness of the text structure strategy and the connection between tasks (e.g., comprehension and composition). Because many textbooks do not make their strategies clear, which

FIGURE 5
Edit/Revise Checklist—Compare/Contrast

Put a question mark (?) on the rough draft where changes are needed.

First Check: Major Ideas	Self-Check		Partner Check	
1. Introduction tells what is being compared	☐ ok	☐ fix	☐ ok	☐ fix
2. Introduction tells theme	☐ ok	☐ fix	☐ ok	☐ fix
3. Differences	☐ ok	☐ fix	☐ ok	☐ fix
4. Similarities	☐ ok	☐ fix	☐ ok	☐ fix
5. Comparison words (like, but, -er)	☐ ok	☐ fix	☐ ok	☐ fix
6. Supporting details	☐ ok	☐ fix	☐ ok	☐ fix

Second Check: Mechanics	Self-Check		Partner Check	
1. Grammar	☐ ok	☐ fix	☐ ok	☐ fix
2. Punctuation	☐ ok	☐ fix	☐ ok	☐ fix
3. Spelling	☐ ok	☐ fix	☐ ok	☐ fix
4. Teacher's Choice	☐ ok	☐ fix	☐ ok	☐ fix

Revision

1. What I like:

2. Needs improvement:

causes difficulties for some students, it may be necessary for teachers to use alternative materials that illustrate text features more explicitly instead of having to rely solely on mainstream curricular materials.

In the example cited, teachers taught compare/contrast text structure using the unit on Canada in social studies. Students identified compare/contrast components and information in chapters on emigration, western expansion, growing industrialization, and modern Canada. Instruction in compare/contrast text structure was integrated with reading comprehension tasks (i.e., identifying and summarizing main ideas and supporting details) and a writing process (i.e., Plan, Organize, Write, Edit, Revise, developed by Englert, Raphael, Anderson, Anthony, and Stevens, [1991]). For students with disabilities, reading expository text and attending to compare/contrast text structure provided content for their compositions and a framework for organizing information.

Primed Background Knowledge

Primed background knowledge is important in reading comprehension. The structure of a reader's preexisting knowledge affects how the student remembers or understands the new knowledge (Weaver & Kintsch, 1991). For expository text structure, research evidence suggests that students who have preexisting awareness of, knowledge of, or sensitivity to text structure demonstrate greater recall of passages than students who do not possess such background knowledge (e.g., Pearson & Fielding, 1991). When teachers or researchers prime or activate background knowledge, they need to consider background knowledge not only of concepts, but also of text structures.

Two approaches were used in the research relating to primed background knowledge of text structure. First, before students read, teachers helped them attend to text structure by displaying graphic or advance organizers that revealed the hierarchical relations between main ideas (Horton, Lovitt, & Bergerud, 1990; Pearson & Fielding, 1991). Second, in the compare/contrast literature (Dickson, 1994; Raphael & Kirschner, 1985; Weisberg & Balaithy, 1989), teachers explicitly taught the elements and organizational patterns of compare/contrast text structure. In the Dickson (1994) study, students applied their newly acquired background knowledge of the components of compare/contrast structure by reorganizing poorly written text to indicate the relations between main ideas and supporting details and producing compare/contrast essays.

Judicious Review

Judicious review refers to the sequence and schedule of opportunities designed to develop facility with the organizational patterns of text structures. In the Dickson study (1994), each lesson began with a review of the new knowledge taught the previous 2 days and ended with a review of the knowledge taught in that lesson. Moreover, the design of instruction systematically applied newly acquired concepts (e.g., compare/contrast components) to more difficult tasks. Students progressed from identifying components of well-written passages to identifying and improving weak passages in their textbooks and finally to composing their own passages. Facility with the components in one task became the prerequisite to success in later applications.

5

Conclusion

The instructional dimensions and adaptation profiles given in the phonological awareness and compare/contrast text structure examples were intended to communicate (a) the available knowledge base in the instructional and curricular requirements for students with disabilities and (b) the complexity of designing instruction to ensure cognitive access for all students in general education.

At present, few commercially available curricular programs are designed carefully or systematically enough to enable students with disabilities to realize their potential or achieve acceptable levels of performance in the general education curriculum without added effort on the part of the teacher. The six principles described in this volume are offered as a starting point to assist general educators in their efforts to provide cognitive access to all students.

The difficulty of adapting inadequately designed curricular materials, nonetheless, requires a two-pronged initiative. First, if students with disabilities are to achieve adequately in the general education curriculum, publishers must recognize and address these principles in programs *prior* to publication. The number of students who cannot access general education content easily or adequately continues to increase; publishers must recognize that students with diverse learning needs are no longer the exception. Proactive efforts must be made to provide well-designed materials that honor the knowledge base of instructional design.

Second, educators must become more knowledgeable in the types of adaptations that are likely to produce significant effects in student learning. This working knowledge will serve two purposes: (1) to allow teachers to evaluate the adequacy of the architecture of instruc-

FIGURE 6
Determining the Adequacy of the Curriculum

1. What percentage of children in your class would be able to perform the skill/strategy, given the existing instruction, at 80% accuracy or above?

2. Considering the full range of learners in your class, what is the overall adequacy of the lesson?

1	2	3	4	5

Highly inadequate   Highly adequate

3. How confident are you that you could modify the lesson to make the information learnable for the range of learners in your class?

1	2	3	4	5

Not confident   Somewhat confident   Very confident

4. Identify the primary modifications you would make in the lessons.

tional materials prior to adoption of materials and (2) to be used as a means of modifying curricular and instructional materials.

The six principles described here are intended to provide educators with the essential knowledge to make the general education content accessible to students with disabilities. Ideally, the cognitive ramps and scaffolds would be part of the original construction, and teachers would merely have to implement these accommodations. Nonetheless, educators can do much to increase the cognitive accessibility of content by attending to the six-principle framework.

As a starting point, we recommend that you answer the questions presented in Figure 6 to determine the adequacy of your curriculum and the extent of adaptations that it may be necessary for you to make. Next, use the six principles to guide your adaptations.

Bibliography and References

Armbruster, B., & Ostertag, J. (1993). Questions in elementary science and social studies textbooks. In B. K. Britton, A. Woodward, & M. Binkley (Eds.), *Learning from textbooks: Theory and practice* (pp. 69–64). Hillsdale, NJ: Erlbaum.

Baker, J., & Zigmond, N. (1990). Are regular education classes equipped to accommodate students with learning disabilities? *Exceptional Children, 56,* 515–526.

Baker, S., Simmons, D., & Kame'enui, E. (1994). Making information more memorable for students with learning disabilities. *Learning Disabilities Forum, 19,* 14–18.

Beck, I. L., McKeown, M. G., & Gromoll, E. W. (1989). Learning from social studies texts. *Cognition and Instruction, 12,* 118–132.

Brophy, J. (1990). Teaching social studies for understanding and higher-order applications. *The Elementary School Journal, 90,* 353–417.

Carnine, D. (1993, December 8). Facts, not fads. *Education Week,* p. 40.

Carnine, D. (1994). Introduction to the mini-series: Educational tools for diverse learners. *School Psychology Review, 32,* 341–350.

Carnine, D. W., Dixon, R., & Kame'enui, E. J. (1994). Math curriculum guidelines for diverse learners. *Curriculum/Technology Quarterly, 3*(3), 1–3.

Carnine, D., Jones, E. D., & Dixon, B. (1994). Mathematics: Educational tools for diverse learners. *School Psychology Review, 23,* 406–427.

Carnine, D., & Kinder D. (1985). Teaching low-performing students to apply generative and schema strategies to narrative and expository material. *Remedial and Special Education, 6,* 20–30.

Carnine, D., Miller, S., Bean, R., & Zigmond, N. (1994). Social studies: Educational tools for diverse learners. *School Psychology Review, 23,* 428–441.

Carroll, J. B. (1963). A model of school learning. *Teachers College Record, 64,* 723–733.

Committee on the Prevention of Reading Difficulties in Young Children. (1998). *Preventing reading difficulties in young children.* (National Research Council Report). Washington, DC: National Academy Press.

Dempster, F. N. (1991). Synthesis of research on reviews and tests. *Educational Leadership, 48,* 71–76.

Dickson, S. (1994). *An examination of the effects of an integrated reading and writing instructional approach on the ability of middle school students to produce and comprehend compare/contrast prose.* Unpublished doctoral dissertation, University of Oregon, Eugene.

Dickson, S. V., Simmons, D. C., & Kame'enui, E. J. (1998). Text organization: Research bases. In D. C. Simmons & E. J. Kame'enui (Eds), *What reading research tells us about children with diverse learning needs* (pp. 239–278). Mahwah, NJ: Erlbaum.

Diegmueller, K. (1995, June 14). California plotting new tack on language arts. *Education Week,* p. 1.

Dimino, J., Gersten, R., Carnine, D., & Blake, G. (1990). Story grammar: An approach for promoting at-risk secondary students' comprehension of literature. *The Elementary School Journal, 91,* 19–32.

Dixon, B., & Carnine, D. (1993). The hazards of poorly designed instructional tools. *Learning Disabilities Forum, 18*(3), 18–22.

Dixon, R., Carnine, D. W., & Kame'enui, E. J. (1992). Curriculum guidelines for diverse learners [Monograph]. Eugene: University of Oregon, National Center to Improve the Tools of Educators.

Engelmann, S., & Carnine, D. W. (1982). *Theory of instruction: Principles and applications.* New York: Irvington.

Englert, C. S., Raphael, T. E., Anderson, L. M., Anthony, H. M., & Stevens, D. D. (1991). Making strategies and self-talk visible: Writing instruction in regular and special education classrooms. *American Educational Research Journal, 2,* 337–372.

Frymier, J., Barber, L., Carriedo, R., Denton, W., Gansneder, B., Johnson-Lewis, S., & Robertson, N. (1992). *Growing up is risky business and schools are not to blame.* Bloomington, IN: Phi Delta Kappa.

Fuchs, D., & Fuchs, L. (1994). Classwide curriculum-based measurement: Helping general educators meet the challenge of student diversity. *Exceptional Children, 60,* 518–537.

Gickling, E., & Thompson, V. (1985). A personal view of curriculum-based assessment. *Exceptional Children, 52,* 219–232.

Gilhool, T. (1973). Education: An inalienable right. *Exceptional Children, 39,* 597–609.

Graham, S., & Harris, K. R. (1989). A components analysis of cognitive strategy instruction: Effects on learning disabled students' compositions and self-efficacy. *Journal of Educational Psychology, 81,* 356–361.

Graves, A., Montague, M., & Wong, Y. (1990). The effects of procedural facilitation on the story composition of learning disabled students. *Learning Disabilities Research, 5,* 88–93.

Hoffman, J. V., McCarthey, S., Abbot, C., Corman, L., Dressman, M., Elliott, B., Matherne, D., & Stahle, D. (1994). So what's new in the new basals? A focus on first grade. *Journal of Reading Behavior, 26,* 47–73.

Horton, S. V., Lovitt, T. C., & Bergerud, D. (1980). The effectiveness of graphic organizers for three classifications of secondary students in content area classes. *Journal of Learning Disabilities, 23,* 12–22.

International math and science study finds U.S. covers more in less depth. (1994, June 24). *Education Week,* p. 10.

Juel, C. (1998). Learning to read and write: A longitudinal study of 54 children from first through fourth grades. *Journal of Educational Psychology, 80,* 437–447.

Kauffman, J. M. (1994). Places of change: Special education's power and identity in an era of educational reform. *Journal of Learning Disabilities, 27,* 610–618.

Kauffman, J. M., & Hallahan, D. P. (1997). A diversity of restrictive environments: Placement as a problem of social ecology. In J. Lloyd, E. J. Kame'enui, & D. Chard (Eds.), *Issues in educating students with disabilities* (pp. 325–342). Mahwah, NJ: Erlbaum.

Kame'enui, E. J. (1993). Diverse learners and the tyranny of time: Don't fix blame; fix the leaky roof. *The Reading Teacher, 46,* 376–383.

Kame'enui, E. J., Carnine, D. W., & Dixon R. C. (1998). Effective teaching strategies that accommodate diverse learners. In E. J. Kame'enui & D. W. Carnine (Eds.), *Effective teaching strategies that accommodate diverse learners* (pp. 1–17). Columbus, OH: Merrill.

Kame'enui, E. J., & Simmons, D. C. (1990). *Designing instructional strategies: The prevention of academic learning problems.* Columbus, OH: Merrill.

Kinder, D., & Bursuck W. (1991). The search for a unified social studies curriculum: Does history really repeat itself? *Journal of Learning Disabilities, 24,* 270–275.

Langer, J., & Applebee, A. (1986). Reading and writing instruction: Toward a theory of teaching and learning. In E. Rothkopf (Ed.), *Review of research in education* (Vol. 13, pp. 171–194). Washington, DC: American Educational Research Association.

Longstreet, W. S., & Shane, H. G. (1993). *Curriculum for a new millennium.* Boston: Allyn & Bacon.

Mayer, R., Sims, V., & Tajika, H. (1995). A comparison of how textbooks test mathematical problem solving in Japan and the United States. *American Educational Research Journal, 32,* 443–460.

McLeskey, J., & Pacchiano, D. (1994). Mainstreaming students with learning disabilities: Are we making progress? *Exceptional Children, 60,* 508–517.

Mosenthal, P. (1982). Designing training programs for learning disabled children: An ideological perspective. *Topics in Learning and Learning Disabilities, 2,* 9–107.

Nezworski, T., Stein, N. L., & Trabasso, T. (1982). Story structure versus content in children's recall. *Journal of Verbal Learning and Verbal Behavior, 21,* 196–206.

Nolet, V., & Tindal, G. (1994). Instruction and learning in middle school science classes: Implications for students with disabilities. *The Journal of Special Education, 28,* 166–187.

Noyce, R. M., & Christie, J. F. (1985). Effects of an integrated approach to grammar instruction on third graders' reading and writing. *The Elementary School Journal, 84,* 63–69.

Pearson, P. D., & Fielding, L. (1991). Comprehension instruction. In R. Barr, M. L. Kamil, P. Mosenthal, & P. D. Pearson (Eds.), *Handbook of reading research* (pp. 815–860). White Plains, NY: Longman.

Porter, A. C. (1989, June–July). A curriculum out of balance: The case of elementary school mathematics. *Educational Researcher, 18*(5), 9–15.

Raphael, T. E., & Kirschner, B. M. (1985). *The effects of instruction in compare/contrast text structure on sixth-grade students' reading comprehension and writing products* (Research Series No. 161). Michigan State University.

Reading scores for high school seniors show drop. (1995, April). *The Register Guard*, p. A7.

Scardamalia, M., & Bereiter, C. (1986). Research on written composition. In M. C. Wittrock (Ed.), *Handbook of research on education* (3rd ed., pp. 778–803). New York: Macmillan.

Shanahan, T., & Lomax, R. G. (1986). An analysis and comparison of theoretical models of the reading–writing relationship. *Journal of Educational Psychology, 78,* 116–123.

Simmons, D. C., Gleason, M. M., Smith, S. B., Baker, S. K., Sprick, M., Thomas, C., Gunn, B., Chard, D., Plasencia-Peinado, J., Peinado, R., & Kame'enui, E. J. (1995, April). *Applications of phonological awareness research in basal reading programs: Evidence and implications for students with reading disabilities.* Paper presented at the meeting of the American Educational Research Association, San Francisco, CA.

Simmons, D. C., & Kame'enui, E. J. (1996). A focus on curriculum design: When children fail. *Focus on Exceptional Children, 28(7),* 1–16.

Simmons, D., Kame'enui, E. J., Dickson, S., Chard, D., Gunn, B., & Baker, S. (1994). Integrating narrative reading and writing instruction for all learners. *Yearbook of the National Reading Council, 43,* 572–582.

Smith, P. L., & Ragan, T. L. (1993). *Instructional design.* New York: Merrill.

Smith, S. B., Simmons, D. C., Gleason, M. M., Kame'enui, E. J., & Baker, S. K. (in press). An analysis of phonological awareness instruction in four kindergarten basal reading programs. *Reading & Writing Quarterly.*

Smith, S., Simmons, D. C., & Kame'enui, E. J. (1998). Phonological awareness: Research bases. In D. C. Simmons & E. J. Kame'enui (Eds.), *What reading research tells us about children with diverse learning needs: Bases and basics* (pp. 129–140). Mahwah, NJ: Erlbaum.

Stanovich, K. E. (1986). Matthew effects in reading: Some consequences of individual differences in the acquisition of literacy. *Reading Research Quarterly, 21,* 360–406.

Tennyson, R., & Christensen, D. L. (1986, April). *Memory theory and design of intelligent learning systems.* Paper presented at the meeting of the American Educational Research Association, San Francisco, CA.

Tierney, R. J., & Shanahan, T. (1991). Research on the reading–writing relationship: Interactions, transactions, and outcomes. In R. Barr,

M. Kamil, P. B. Mosenthal, & P. D. Pearson (Eds.), *Handbook of reading research* (Vol. 2, pp. 246–280). New York: Longman.

Torgesen, J. K., Wagner, & Rashotte, C. (1994). Longitudinal studies of phonological processing and reading. *Journal of Learning Disabilities, 27,* 276–286.

U.S. Department of Education. (1994). *Sixteenth annual report to Congress on the implementation of the Individuals with Disabilities Education Act.* Washington, DC: Author.

Weaver, C. A., III, & Kintsch, W. (1991). Expository text. In R. Barr, M. L. Kamil, P. Mosenthal, & P. D. Pearson (Eds.), *Handbook of reading research* (pp. 230–244). White Plaines, NY: Longman.

Weisberg, R., & Balaithy, E. (1989, May–June). *Effects of topic familiarity and training in generative learning activities on poor readers' comprehension of comparison/contrast expository text structure: Transfer to real-word materials.* Paper presented at the Annual Meeting of the International Reading Association, New Orleans, Louisiana.

Worrall, R. S., & Carnine, D. (1994, March). *Lack of professional support undermines teachers and reform—A contrasting perspective from health and engineering.* Unpublished manuscript, National Center to Improve the Tools of Educators, College of Education, University of Oregon, Eugene.

Yopp, H. K. (1988). The validity and reliability of phonemic awareness tests. *Reading Research Quarterly, 23,* 159–177.

Zigmond, N., Jenkins, J., Fuchs, L. S., Deno, S., Fuchs, D., Baker, J. N., Jenkins, L., & Couthino, M. (1995). Special education in restructured schools: Findings from three multi-year studies. *Phi Delta Kappan, 76,* 531–540.